The Indian Ocean

To the first explorers, the Indian Ocean represented the gateway to the unlimited riches of the east. And indeed, this is one of the most interesting and colourful of the oceans of the world. Stretching from the Arabian Sea in the north-west, through the tropics to the icy Antarctic in the south, the Indian Ocean is bordered by a huge variety of different countries. Scattered across its warm waters are hundreds of sun-drenched islands with palm-fringed beaches and beautiful coral reefs. With the aid of sixty pictures and diagrams, this book tells you something about the upheavals within the Earth which caused the formation of the Indian Ocean millions of years ago, the wildlife that lives in and around its waters, and the way man is harvesting many of its resources. You can also learn about the beautiful coral reefs that surround many of the islands, and the graceful sailing *dhows* which crisscross the ocean with the seasonal monsoons. At the back you will find a glossary, index and reading list.

SEAS AND OCEANS

The Indian Ocean

Edited by Pat Hargreaves

WAYLAND

SILVER BURDETT

© Copyright 1981 Wayland Publishers Ltd
First published in 1981 by
Wayland (Publishers) Limited
61 Western Road, Hove,
East Sussex BN3 1JD, England

Published in the United States by
Silver Burdett Press
Morristown, New Jersey
1987 printing

Phototypeset by
Direct Image Photosetting, Hove, Sussex
Printed in Italy by
G. Canale & C. S.p.A., Turin

Library of Congress Cataloging-in-Publication Data

The Indian Ocean.

(Seas and oceans)
Bibliography: p. [72].
Includes index.
Summary: An introduction to the Indian Ocean, discussing its formation, exploration, plant and animal life, resources, and trade routes. Includes glossary.
1. Indian Ocean–Juvenile literature. [1. Indian Ocean] I. Hargreaves, Pat. II. Series.
GC721.I49   1986   910'.09182'4   86-29844
ISBN 0-382-06582-4 (Silver Burdett)

Seas and Oceans

Three-quarters of the earth's surface is covered by sea. Each book in this series takes you on a cruise of a mighty ocean, telling you of its history, discovery and exploration, the people who live on its shores, and the animals and plants found in and around it.

The Atlantic
The Caribbean and Gulf of Mexico
The Mediterranean
The Antarctic
The Arctic
The Indian Ocean
The Red Sea and Persian Gulf
The Pacific

Contents

1 A JOURNEY AROUND THE INDIAN OCEAN

Of all the oceans in the world the Indian Ocean is possibly the most fascinating. It is an ocean of extremes, with a climate which varies from the steamy heat of the tropics to the icy cold of the south where it meets Antarctic waters. For many hundreds of years explorers and traders have crisscrossed this magnificent ocean, plying their trade along its shores. The discovery of its riches by Europeans in the fifteenth century is a story of courage, shipwrecks, treasure and piracy. But its interest lies not only in the stories of past ages. Today scientific expeditions are learning more about the secrets of this vast ocean. Scientists study the many species of marine plants and animals which live in its waters. They study the rocks which form the sea floor, and measure volcanic activity. They also monitor the notorious seasonal monsoons, and calculate their effect on water currents and waves.

If you look on the map you will see that the continent of Africa forms a long western boundary to the Indian Ocean. Halfway up

Below An Arab *dhow* under full sail. These ships have plyed their trade across this Ocean for centuries.

Above Fishermen ride the waves in a small dugout canoe.

the coast is the large tropical island of Madagascar, with its unique form of animal life — including giant tortoises. Further up the coast we come to the 'horn of Africa' — the hot, baking, desert-like lands of Somalia and Ethiopia, which are frequently afflicted by terrible droughts. To the north you will see the Arabian Sea, the Red Sea and Persian Gulf, surrounded by various Middle East countries. At the far end of the Red Sea is the famous Suez Canal. Every year hundreds of ships take this short cut through to the Mediterranean.

The Arabian Sea is bordered by the Arab Sultanate of Oman, Pakistan, and India. India has many resources but is also one of the most densely populated countries in the world. Off the south coast of India lies the

Above The Indian Ocean borders the hot, arid lands of the 'horn of Africa'. Camels rest near an oasis by the shore.
Below Fishermen haul up the sail of their *dhow*.

beautiful island of Sri Lanka from which gemstones, tea and spices are exported. To the east of India is the Bay of Bengal, with Bangladesh to the north and Burma on its eastern shore. Fierce storms may sometimes sweep up the Bay of Bengal causing serious flooding around the north of the Ganges in Bangladesh.

On the eastern borders of the ocean and further to the south are the warm, beautiful and mysterious islands of Java and Sumatra. Between the two islands lies the island of Krakatoa, which exploded in a gigantic volcanic eruption in 1883. If we continue southwards we reach Australia and Tasmania. Far to the south is the cold, windy Antarctic Ocean. In these polar seas, the Indian Ocean meets the Pacific to the east and the Atlantic to the west. In the cold Antarctic there may even be icebergs.

Dotted across the Indian Ocean, often separated by hundreds of miles of sea, are many groups of beautiful islands. Places like Zanzibar with its Arab architecture and big sea-going dhows, the Seychelles, famous for their huge coconut palms, the Maldives with their beautiful coral atolls, and the Nicobar Islands which were once the home of pirates. In the southern part of the ocean lie the windswept Crozets and Kerguelen Isles — not very hospitable to man, but enjoyed by large colonies of seals and sea birds.

Right Map of the Indian Ocean. The different depths of the ocean are indicated by different shades of blue — the darkest blue represents the deepest water.

A S I A

AFRICA

ARABIAN
SEA

BAY
OF
BENGAL

Sri Lanka

Maldive
Is.

Seychelles

Zanzibar

Madagascar

AUSTRALIA

Crozet
Is.

Kerguelen
Is.

ANTARCTICA

2 HOW THE INDIAN OCEAN WAS FORMED

Underwater mountain chains

If you look at the map of the sea floor of the Indian Ocean, the most striking thing you notice is that a mountain chain occupies its centre in the shape of an 'upside-down Y'. The two lower arms run from the centre of the ocean, one passing south of Africa and the other passing south of Australia. The shorter upper arm passes into the Red Sea between Africa and Arabia. This mountain chain is a long line of undersea peaks that stand about two thousand metres above the deep ocean basins on either side. All along its length are volcanoes erupting new rock on to the deep sea floor, causing the whole chain to be a belt where earthquakes are frequently recorded. The chain, or mid-ocean ridge system, is where new sea floor is continually being added on either side, so that the whole ocean is constantly becoming wider. This spreading apart of the floor of the oceans, when new material is added at the centre, happens at a rate of only one and a half to three centimetres (½-1 in) of movement each year. But over millions of years the continents around the edge of the Indian Ocean have been pushed further and further apart.

The continents of Africa, India, Australia and Antarctica, were once part of a single super-continent known as Gondwanaland. This landmass began to break up about 130 to 140 million years ago, when the volcanic ridge system first broke through between Africa and Antarctica. This was followed, about 110 million years ago, by the drifting apart of India and the still-joined Australia and Antarctica. All the time the basins on either side of the ridge system were getting deeper and wider. The last continental break-up occurred around 40 million years ago, when the spreading that was happening between India and northern Australia switched to the south of Australia, and a seaway opened up between this continent and Antarctica. Today Africa and Arabia are moving apart at the rate of one centimetre (½ in) per year as the Red Sea widens.

Right Artist's impression of the Indian Ocean drained of its water. You can see the mountain ranges, ridges and deep trenches which make up the sea floor. The biggest mountain chain is in the shape of an upside-down Y running down the centre of the map.

Plateaus, trenches and volcanoes

Above A drawing of the volcano of Krakatoa before it blew up in a gigantic explosion in 1883.

Another look at the map of the sea floor shows you that there are a number of other large features beneath the surface of the Indian Ocean, as well as the spreading ridge and the deep basin plains.

During the continental break-up and spreading, small pieces of continent were left behind in the wake of the drifting landmasses. These fragments remain as plateaus, mostly below the sea surface. However in places their highest points appear as small island groups, such as the Seychelles.

All around the Pacific Ocean there are areas where the ocean floor is thought to be slipping beneath the surrounding continents. Here the earth's crust is bent downwards and very deep ocean trenches are formed. These places represent the deepest parts of the world's oceans. In the Indian Ocean only one

of these trenches is known. This is the Java Trench which curves around the south of Indonesia, reaching a depth of over seven kilometres (4½ miles), at its deepest part. This trench has been in existence only for about the last 20 million years of the Indian Ocean's history. Most of the oldest ocean floor has still not slipped below the continents. The constant slippage of one piece of the earth under another causes volcanic activity. The trench is bordered to the north by a line of large island volcanoes. In 1883 one of these, Krakatoa, blew up in an enormous explosion, and the dust from this coloured sunsets all over the world for a year after the event.

Apart from the mid-ocean ridge system, there are a number of other long ridges stretching across the Indian Ocean floor. As with the plateaus these lie mostly below the surface, but in some places, such as the Laccadive Islands, they rise above the sea. These other ridges are not affected by earthquakes and are thought to have formed at an angle to the main spreading ridge.

Below Lava flows in a volcanic crater on the island of Java.

Submarine fans

Submarine fans are huge thicknesses of sediment spread out on the ocean floor by major rivers. Because the enormous input of sediment eroded from the land far exceeds the normal distribution of sediments by the ocean currents, most of the material is deposited within a few hundred kilometres of where the river water enters. The two river systems of the world which carry the largest amounts of material to the ocean are the Ganges and the Indus systems. Both pour their waters into the northern Indian Ocean. Southern Africa's largest river, the Zambezi, brings its sediment load into the ocean near Madagascar. All three have built up thicknesses of thousands of metres of sediment near the river's mouth and delta, and a fan extends in a wedge shape which spreads away from this source. The Indus Fan covers almost all of the Arabian Sea north of the spreading ridge, while the Bengal Fan is even larger, extending right down to the central parts of the ocean. Much of the sediment spread over the surfaces of these fans enters from the river delta edge as short-lived underwater avalanches. Over thousands of years these avalanches have followed well-worn tracks and have developed channel systems which decorate the surface of the fans, rather like river systems do over some land areas.

Left Rock samples from the ocean floor are dredged up by scientists for examination.

Above The crowded waters of the River Ganges. The Ganges deposits enormous quanitities of sediment into the Indian Ocean.

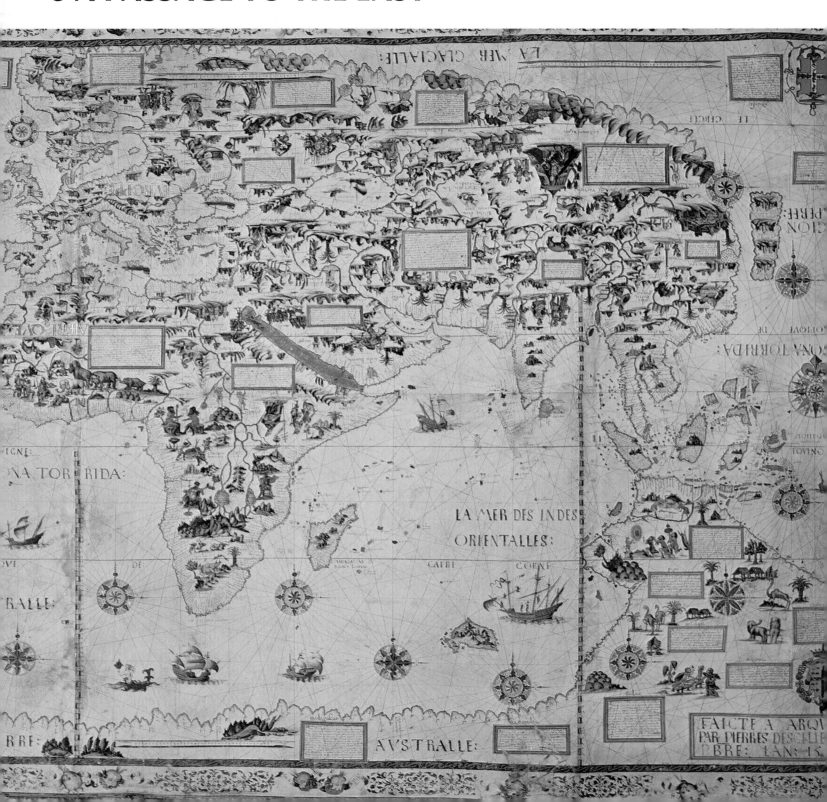

Today when a man is sent into space, it cannot be certain what he will find. He is charting new territory. The same is true of the explorers who, centuries ago, set out to discover new lands at the farthest corners of the earth. Nowadays every part of the Indian Ocean is known, and ships from all over the world plough to and fro across its waters.

But in the fifteenth century, the pioneers who sailed from the sanctuary of Portugal's ports had no accurate maps to guide them, and no real knowledge of what to expect. Navigational aids were so crude that captains often preferred to follow the stars — and their own instincts. Many sailors were still afraid that they might sail over a gigantic waterfall at the edge of the earth.

The early explorers were inspired by news of the splendour of the East, which gradually filtered back to Europe as a result of the overland travels of men like Marco Polo. This great Italian explorer and trader painted a picture of the East as the treasure house of the world, an eternal source of fabulous wealth. Not surprisingly, European kings hoped to get their hands on some of these riches. The first expeditions were motivated by greed, curiosity and a crusading zeal which wished to make Christianity the universal religion. Most important of all was the desire for trade, particularly in spices. Up until then this trade had been controlled by the Arabs.

Above Vasco da Gama is received by the ruler of Calicut after his pioneering voyage across the Indian Ocean.

Right A fifteenth century Portuguese sailing ship.

Left A French sixteenth-century map drawn specially for seafarers. On such charts the lettering and illustration in the northern hemisphere were often put in upside down.

17

Above Malaysian spice merchants on the island of Java. Notice the European warship in the bay.

Successive kings of Portugal, from Prince Henry the Navigator onwards, were fascinated by the Indian Ocean. The knowledge collected by Prince Henry at his School of Navigation, provided the inspiration for Portuguese ships to press further and further down the Atlantic coast of Africa, in an attempt to find a new way to the East. Henry died in 1460, but his successors continued the search. The crucial breakthrough came in 1488, when Bartolomeu Diaz rounded the Cape of Good Hope, and proved that there was no land obstacle blocking the path to the East. Armed with this knowledge, Vasco da Gama led an expedition to establish trading links with the natives of the countries on the shores of the Indian Ocean. The fleet sailed from Portugal in 1497 with a complement of 170 men aboard four ships. In May, 1498, he reached India, and forced a trading agreement on the local ruler, the Zamorin of Calicut. His dealings with the Indians established a pattern of cruelty and arrogance that the Dutch and English found regrettably easy to follow. This ruthless approach formed the basis of the Portuguese Empire in the Indian Ocean which lasted unchallenged for over a century.

This monopoly was broken when Dutch and English explorers also began to appear in the East. Both created their own long-lasting empires, in the Dutch East Indies and the Indian sub-continent respectively. But the credit for the opening up of the Indian Ocean must go to the early Portuguese explorers, some of whom lost their lives in the search for the wonders of the East.

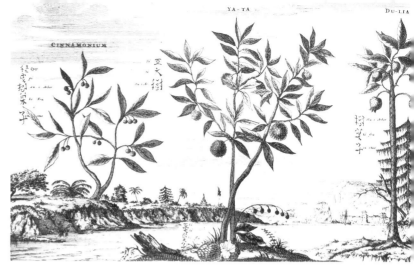

Above A seventeenth century drawing of some of the valuable spices grown in the East Indies.

Above A show of strength by the British in the Indian Ocean. A fleet bombards the port of Muscat.

4 MONSOONS AND THE SEA
Climate, temperature and salinity

The presence of vast continental landmasses to the north of the Indian Ocean help to determine its climate. The most outstanding features of this climate are the monsoon winds (from an Arab word meaning 'seasonal') which affects both the land and the sea, north of the line of latitude 10° south. From November to March, the cool, dry

North-East Monsoon blows down from the Asian Continent and across the ocean; from May to September the warm, humid winds of the South-West Monsoon blow in the opposite direction back towards Asia. As they rise over the mountains north of the Bay of Bengal they cause heavy rainfall. This may result in serious flooding in Bangladesh around the mouth of the Ganges (also caused by fierce storms, see page 24). In contrast to these dramatic seasonal variations, the trade winds in the southern part of the ocean blow from the south-east all the year round.

Over most of the Indian Ocean, climatic conditions are tropical. Temperatures are usually over 18°C, and can be as high as 30°C near the equator. In extreme southern latitudes, though, conditions are very much colder. The average annual rainfall over the Ocean is about 1000 millimetres (40 inches), which is about the same as southern England. However, levels of rainfall vary tremendously from place to place — from less than 250 millimetres (10 inches) off the desert lands surrounding the Arabian Sea, to 3000 millimetres (120 inches) off the coast of tropical Sumatra.

The surface waters of the Indian Ocean are heated by the sun to temperatures that vary between about 30°C at its warmest part in the Arabian Sea to less than 12°C south of

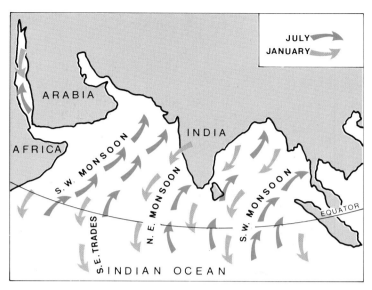

Above The monsoons blow for six months from the north-east and six months from the south-west every year without fail.

latitude 40°S. The temperature is very much colder below the surface of the sea. Even at the equator, where the surface water is very warm, the water approximately one kilometre (½ a mile) down will be very cool, and the water at the bottom (at 3 kilometres or deeper) may be as cold as 2°C.

The amount of salt in the water changes a little according to the depth of the water and its distance from the Poles. These variations in salinity are very slight and range from about 36.5 grammes (1.25 oz) of salt per 1000 grammes (35.2 oz) of water in the Arabian Sea (that is the same as dissolving about two level teaspoons of salt in half a litre — about a pint — of water) to 34 grammes per 1000 near the Antarctic.

Left Two Indian women shelter under an umbrella with their belongings during the worst of the monsoon rains.

Currents

Above This instrument is used to measure the movements of currents.

The main cause of ocean surface currents is the frictional drag of the wind on the water. In the southern part of the Indian Ocean the south-east winds cause an anticlockwise circulation of water all the year round.

Along the south-west shore of the ocean, the strong Agulhas Current flows southwards between Africa and Madagascar. This current turns east when it reaches a latitude of about 35° south to complete the anticlockwise circle of the southern Indian Ocean. In the north the variations of the monsoon winds cause seasonal changes of the currents. From about November to March, the north-east winds produce the North Equatorial Current which flows westwards just north of the equator. However, from about May to September, when the South-West Monsoon blows, the North Equatorial Current disappears, and there is a general eastward flow of water across the centre of the ocean. There are also a number of deep-water currents that flow below the surface of the Indian Ocean.

The directions of the winds, and probably of the currents also, have been known to sailors for hundreds of years. Trading *dhows* from the Arabian states planned their voyages with the seasonal monsoons in mind. You can read more about these voyages and the boats they sailed in on page 58.

Right Ocean-going *dhows* still use the winds and currents in their voyages up and down the African coast.

Tides

Shortly after the ocean tide level outside the Aldabra coral atoll has reached its lowest level, you can see the triangular-shaped shark fins breaking the surface as they gather outside a shallow entrance channel. The sharks' built-in tide tables tell them that water will soon begin to flow strongly back into the lagoon as the levels rise. When the water in the channel is deep enough they will swim into the lagoon to prey on fish and other rich marine life.

For lagoons like Aldabra the regular twice-daily filling by the tides also brings in water, rich in oxygen and nutrients, which help to support the marine life within the lagoon. Animals which live on the reef flats must also adjust to the regular tidal flooding by the sea. Those species which adjust best, have the greatest chance of survival. At the low levels, which are flooded for most of the time, the species which do well are quite different from those which thrive at the high levels, which are only flooded for short periods, at high tide.

People who live on low-lying land near the sea must also adapt to its ways. On the fertile muddy land at the mouth of the River Ganges

Below Sharks accompany the incoming tide to prey on the rich marine life of the coral reefs.

Above Flooding in Bangladesh following a hurricane in the Bay of Bengal.

the people of Bangladesh can grow rich crops. But they must beware of the flooding which sometimes happens when hurricane storms sweep up the Bay of Bengal from the equator. These fierce winds can drive the sea waters many miles inland with disastrous results. Satellite pictures are used as part of a monitoring system which aims to give these people reliable warnings in plenty of time.

Another kind of disastrous flooding followed the explosion of the island of Krakatoa, between Java and Sumatra, in 1883. The bang was heard 3000 kilometres away, but the shock water-wave that ensued travelled to all parts of the Indian Ocean, and was also seen as far away as the North Atlantic.

5 LIFE IN THE OPEN SEA
Plants and animals near the surface

In the open sea, far from land, the water is very clear. When the sun shines, the water is warm and very bright down to a depth of about 100 metres (330 ft), and here plants can live. Deeper down it becomes too dark for plants to grow.

Below This jellyfish is called a sea wasp. It is the most poisonous creature in the oceans.

In shallow water, many plants can grow attached to the bottom. But in some parts of the ocean, the sea bed is several kilometres deep so all the plants that live there must float near the surface. Almost all of these are very small and you need a microscope to see them. A quarter of a million may live in one cubic centimetre, and yet, because they are so small the water still looks perfectly clear. They come in many shapes and sizes. Some enclose themselves in tiny cases of a hard chemical such as silicate, taken from the seawater. Others have two whip-like threads which they beat to move through the water. They may be single cells or may grow into long, delicate chains.

As well as light the plants also need special chemicals, which are taken from the water by each cell. The chemicals are called nutrients and where there are a lot of these, such as near a river mouth, the plants grow and multiply much faster.

Because these tiny plants drift, they are called plankton. Almost all life in the open sea depends on them. Many fish eat them, and when the sun shines on them, they make oxygen which is needed by all creatures in the sea.

An important part of the life in shallow water are the animal plankton. These are tiny drifting animals which are bigger than the plant cells, but are still mostly too small to see, without a microscope. Many of them feed on the plant cells. Many are larvae, which are

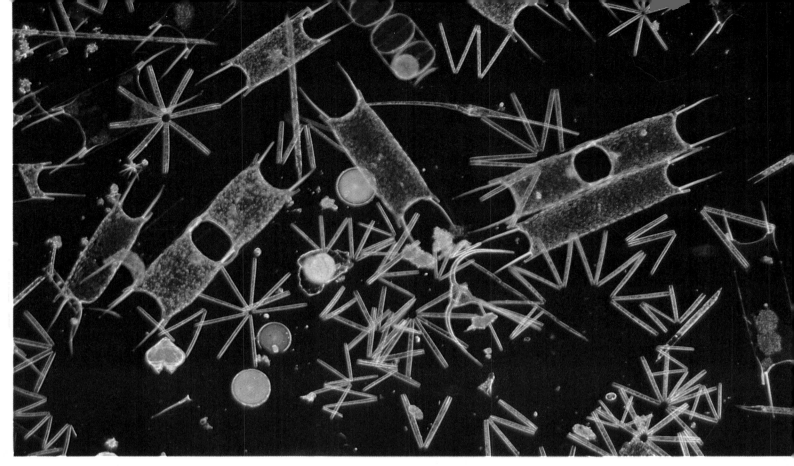

Above Some of the extraordinary plant life that drifts through the oceans. They are vital to almost all life in the ocean as a food source, and as makers of oxygen.

the young of larger animals, such as crabs and starfish. These float and travel long distances before growing into adults. They too are eaten by fish. So many are eaten that the parents need to produce thousands to make sure that some survive.

Some floating animals are quite large. For example jellyfish drift along, trailing tentacles which have many tiny darts on them to sting and poison their prey. Small animals are immediately killed, and even people can be hurt by some of them.

The commonest of the larger animals are the fish. Many fish swim together for safety, in schools of several thousand. Some, like the flying fish, leap out of the water when they are chased by a predator, and when they are in the air they spread their huge fins and glide a long way to safety. Most of the larger fish swim and hunt alone. Sharks are the best known of these and they roam over large areas catching and eating smaller fish. Some of the biggest of all though, the whale shark and the manta ray, feed on the tiny plankton and are harmless.

The deeper layers

Deep down it is dark and cold, even on the equator. No plants can grow here, but the dead and dying remains of plants and animals from the sunlit regions above, fall slowly downwards, and help to provide enough food for many types of deep sea life. Often the fish are strange compared to the familiar shallow water types. Some have bright luminous spots that shine out in the dark. Many have strange shapes. The angler fish sits on the bottom waving a long lure which hangs over its head. Fish are attracted to the lure and are then caught and swallowed. Many fish have enormous mouths so that they can swallow prey that are bigger than themselves. This is because food is so difficult to catch that they may have a long wait before eating again, and one mouthful must last them a long time.

Where there is rock, there are many attached animals, like colourful sea anemones and delicately branching corals which can grow in the darkness. Most of the ocean floor though, is not bare rock but is

Below This fearsome creature, with its long, curving teeth and enormous appetite, is called a viper fish.

Above A beautiful sea anemone, with tentacles extended to capture passing prey.

covered by a layer of fine sediment. This is made from countless tiny grains of rocky or bony material that has settled down from the water above. Some of it comes from rivers a long way away. A lot of it is the remains of plant and animal life which lived in the sunlit region. When these died their tiny skeletons sank into the cold, deep ocean, and over millions of years have formed thick layers of sediment.

Many animals creep over the sediment, feeding on what they can find. Others such as worms burrow into it. Many eat the sediment itself to digest the remaining organic matter. Life exists even in the deepest, darkest and coldest parts of the sea.

6 MAMMALS AND BIRDS OF THE OCEAN

Dugongs and seals

The northern shores of the Indian Ocean are the home of dugongs or sea-cows, strange aquatic mammals like large, sleepy seals, that browse on the sea grasses of shallow coastal waters. Dugongs are leathery animals, with wrinkled skin and sad, bewhiskered faces. Their fore-limbs are flippers and they have no hind legs, so they cannot walk on land. But the tail has double, pointed flukes (paddle-like fins) that push them slowly through the water.

Large, fat creatures, some over three metres (10 ft) long, dugongs weigh 300 kilogrammes (661 lbs) or more — as much as four big men. They move in small groups like herds of cows, from one patch of underwater grass to the next, the calves swimming along with the adults. Their chief enemy is man; a century ago dugongs were plentiful from Africa to Australia, but they are easily caught in nets and many are killed for their meat, fat, and tough hides.

The remote islands of the southern Indian Ocean, cold and rainswept all the year round,

Below An elephant seal bellows angrily. They get their name from the trunk-like nose of the male.

Above A dugong, with its escort of fish, moves gently on to the next feeding ground.

are the haunt of two different kinds of seal — fur seals and elephant seals. The fur seals are lively animals, as much at home on land as in the water. Males grow one and a half to two metres (4-6 ft) long, females are usually smaller, and both are covered with sleek grey-brown or yellowish fur, that helps them to keep warm in the cold seas. The females come ashore in early summer, forming into small groups or harems of five or six that are guarded by the large mature males. Pups born in November or December are fed by their mothers for three to four months. Then they leave the nursery beaches for the sea, where — like their parents — they live on fish, krill and cuttlefish.

Elephant seals too leave the sea to breed on the island beaches. They get their name from their enormous size (a big bull may be over two metres [6 ft] long and weigh four tonnes), and from the trunk-like nose of the male, which he inflates — making him look even bigger — when driving rival bulls away from his harem.

Whales and sea birds

Whales are also found in large numbers in the Indian Ocean, especially in the south where fish and krill are most plentiful. The big whales — blue, fin, sei and sperm — spend their summers feeding and fattening among the rich plankton and fish shoals of the south, even among the ice floes of the Antarctic where food is abundant. Then they swim northwards into warmer tropical waters, where the females give birth to their calves. A newborn whale may be over six metres (20 ft) long and weigh two to three tonnes. Like all other young mammals, whale calves feed on their mother's milk. They grow and fatten very quickly in the warm ocean, and begin to feed themselves for the first time during their long swim southwards in spring. Apart from the big whales, there are also smaller species of whale and dolphin in the Indian Ocean. Some of these are very rare and have only been seen a few times from ships.

The ocean supports many kinds of sea bird, especially around the islands where the water is rich in plankton and fish. The birds feed at

Below The dolphin is the smallest member of the whale family. They are playful creatures, and usually live and hunt together in groups.

sea, then find cliffs, trees and sandy beaches for nesting, on the islands themselves. On the northern islands, tropical species — noddies, boobies, terns and big black frigate birds — breed in nearly every month of the year. They fly off every morning to catch fish or plankton, returning each evening to feed their young in the nest. In the south live a different group of cold-water species, including storm petrels, albatrosses, and penguins. These nest only in summer.

Left This young fellow is a baby booby. His feet seem to be several sizes too large for him.

Below Frigate birds on the Seychelles. The male has a large red pouch which he puffs out when he feels aggressive or romantic.

7 THE SEA SHORES
Rocky and sandy shores

Where the land meets the ocean at the seashore there are many small and colourful animals and plants. Many of the animals that live here cannot live anywhere else. There are rocky shores and sandy shores, and different animals live on each.

In rocky areas you will find molluscs, soft-bodied animals with shells on their backs. These crawl slowly about searching for food.

Small pink and green seaweeds grow on the rocks too, and rock pools contain many types of seaweed, shells and small fish in their clear water. Life on sandy beaches is usually different. The white sand usually comes from ground-up corals. Crabs are common here, running sideways and feeding on rotting plants that have been washed up by the tide. Some burrow into their holes when you go too close, while others dash into the water to hide. Hermit crabs are a very common species. They have soft bodies and so carry a mollusc

Below This hermit crab borrows a mollusc shell to give its soft body protection against predators.

Above Turtle hatchlings emerge from their nest. Many will be eaten by sea birds before they reach the safety of the sea.

shell around to protect themselves. Many sorts of crab live on the shore but all return to the sea to lay their eggs.

One type of animal lives in the sea but crawls out onto the land to lay its eggs. This is the turtle, and there are several types with different colours and patterns on their backs. When she is ready to lay her eggs, the mother drags her heavy body up the beach with her flippers. She digs a hole above the high tide line and lays eggs in it. The young hatch after a few weeks, climb out of the sand and dash down to the water where they swim away.

Sometimes it is very hot on the shore and everything is covered with dried sea salt. At other times it is drenched with rain which can harm some marine animals and plants. Because of this, many animals and plants cannot live here at all, but those species that have adapted successfully to the changing conditions of the sea-shore are usually very common.

Life in the mangrove swamps

Above A mangrove swamp. Notice the stilt-like roots of the trees.

On some shores a special kind of tree grows by the water's edge. It is called the mangrove tree and is found in flat, swampy areas beside the sea and actually in the water itself. The ground around them is usually soft and very muddy and is often flooded by rivers or by the sea. Locations include parts of southern India and South-East Asia.

If a tree is to grow, its roots must have oxygen, just like all living things. But the mud in which the mangrove tree grows often has no oxygen, and so the roots of most other trees find this an impossible place to live. The characteristic mangrove though, has special roots which grow partly out of the mud and up into the air where they can breathe. Each tree has plenty of these roots, and usually many mangrove trees grow close together, so that a dense forest of roots is formed which is almost impossible to walk through.

The roots are important in several ways. They feed the trees and support them on the soft mud. They also prevent the mud from being washed away from the edge of the shore and so prevent erosion of the land.

A great number of animals live in and around the forest of roots. Many fish find shelter amongst them, and one kind behaves very strangely for a fish. This is a creature called the mudskipper. It can climb right out of the water onto the mangrove roots and even into the trees themselves, where it can stay for a long time, holding on to branches with its specially shaped fins. Many crabs scuttle about in the dark jungle of roots, sometimes in and sometimes out of the water. Whelks crawl over the roots, taking care not to fall into the mud. Higher up, birds nest in the branches. An enormous amount of wildlife is found on this type of shore, and all because the mangrove tree is adapted to living in the mud.

Below The extraordinary mudskipper fish climbs right out of the water to bask on the mangrove roots.

8 A CORAL REEF

How the reef is formed

Coral reefs occur in most of the tropical Indian Ocean though not along continental coasts near large river deltas. Corals are animals which are able to build reefs. A kind of algae (plants) are also important, because they cement the coral reefs together, and some can even build parts of a reef themselves. Other animals, such as worms and molluscs with shells, may also contribute. These reef builders grow over and into each other until a large rocky and often cavernous structure is formed, hundreds of metres across. This is the reef framework.

Reefs are the home of hundreds of other forms of life many of which leave behind their

Below Coral reefs and islands in the Maldives.

shells after they die. Others bore into the rocky reef and produce fine fragments as they do so, while the waves and currents break up parts of the reef and wear it down. All this material becomes reef sediment which fills the spaces between the growing reef framework, or accumulates around it. In this way a reef is partly a living, growing structure, and partly an area where plant and animal debris builds up bedded deposits.

Geological events, the weather, and the action of the sea all affect the shape of coral reefs. Changes of sea level are especially important. Sometimes the sea floor on which the reef is growing shifts up or down, and true sea level also changes with time. Either event can leave a once living reef stranded above sea level, or drown it too deeply for reef life to grow properly. When a reef is left above the sea, waves, streams and rainwater acids attack it and carve it into a landscape of gorges, hollows, caves, cliffs and sharply irregular surfaces. There are 'raised reefs' like this along much of the African coast.

Sometimes reefs grow on the shores of volcanic islands. The islands sink over millions of years leaving ring-shaped reefs or 'atolls' as in the Maldives. ('Atoll' is probably the only word in English taken from the Maldive language.)

Right How a coral atoll is formed.

FRINGING REEF

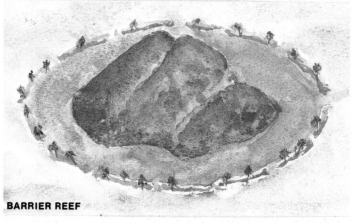

BARRIER REEF

CORAL ATOLL

Life on a reef

Above The beautiful architecture of the corals makes swimming over the reef seem like entering a dream world.

If you set out to explore a typical shore reef, as are found in the Seychelles and Maldives, you must first make the short journey by boat to the reef flats. If you have never visited a reef before, you may be disappointed not to immediately see the colourful coral scenes you have been led to expect. These await you further out, but on the flats you will usually find a rich carpet of sea grasses. These are true flowering plants, not seaweeds, and they trap loose sediment, broken and worn down from the reef rock.

Corals usually appear in deeper, more freely circulating parts of the reef flats, and along reef edges where the flats end and drop away into deeper water. The corals grow in all kinds of rounded and branching shapes, in delicate translucent colours and darker greens and browns. To some people these are the 'coral gardens', but with their spires, columns and dome-shaped colonies, they are more like beautiful cities of fantasy architecture. Where the water is regularly rough however, the towering and delicate corals are replaced by low stunted forms. The reef-building stony seaweeds are often more common in rough water than the coral animals, where they may build up a pink rocky platform.

To see reef life properly, you need to be able to swim underwater with a face mask (make sure you swim in *safe areas*). On almost every part of the reef you will notice an enormous number of fish. Their bright colours, striking patterns and varied shapes and habits all illustrate the great variety of life supported by the reef. Many other creatures stay hidden, but at night, sea urchins, shrimps, lobsters, starfish and feather stars emerge from hiding places to feed and catch prey. During the day they hide beneath boulders and in caves and crevices. Here you will also find a rich covering of brightly coloured sponges and other kinds of animals. In amongst the rocky reef masses are molluscs, worms and crustaceans. Some like bivalves and sponges bore deeply into the rock. Some worms and crabs make their homes in the living coral, which gradually grow round them to give protection.

Many forms of reef life have sharing relationships (symbiosis). Perhaps the most important of these are the minute single-celled plants which live within the coral tissue, and share with it some of the important substances which are in short supply in shallow tropical ocean water (nitrogen and phosphorus). This sharing seems to make the corals able to grow faster and larger, and so to be more effective reef builders. This in turn helps to provide more places for other reef inhabitants to live, and explains the great variety of reef life.

Above All kinds of different creatures inhabit the nooks and crannies of the reef. Here a blue damsel fish swims past two cleaner shrimps.

9 EXPLORING THE ISLANDS

The Seychelles

There are hundreds of beautiful islands scattered across the warm waters of the Indian Ocean. Many of them are coral or volcanic in nature and range in size from the large tropical island of Madagascar, which is almost 16,000 kilometres (995 miles) in length, to the smallest coral atoll of the Maldive Islands.

Particularly attractive are the islands of the Seychelles. Totalling some 90 islands, they are dotted across 1,000 kilometres (625 miles) of ocean. The main group represents the tips of a sunken continental fragment and centres on the island of Mahé. This accounts for a third of the country's area and 95 per cent of the population. The outlying islands are coral, built on outcrops of the underwater ridge that stretches southwards across the ocean towards the islands of Mauritius and Réunion.

Below Children with fish traps on a beach in the Seychelles. The whiteness of the sand is dazzling.

Above Enormous coconuts of the unique palm tree 'coco du mer' on the island of Praslin.

Astonishingly, the beautiful, well-watered island of Mahé was uninhabited when French settlers from Mauritius colonized it, and neighbouring islands of the main group, in the mid-eighteenth century. These early settlers were in search of lands for spice-growing, and they brought with them slaves of African origin. These attempts to cultivate spices were only partially successful, though to this day cinnamon-leaf, oil and vanilla are among the crops the islands export.

Sadly, this early land clearance stripped the mountains of their original high rainforest. Only on the island of Praslin is there a small clump of the unique 'coco du mer' — a palm tree of enormous size, which takes 40 years to come to fruit and whose huge, nine kilogramme (20 lb) coconuts take seven years to mature.

The principal industry today is copra — the dried oil-yielding kernel of the coconut. It is

43

grown both on the islands of the main group and also, with the help of imported labour, on the outlying islands. The small boats which service the distant islands also catch large quantities of fish from the rich grounds that lie between the Seychelles and Mauritius.

French authority over the Seychelles ended with the Napoleonic wars, when the islands came under British rule in 1814. However, French influence is still strong today, particularly in the Creole dialect which is the tongue of the many coloured peoples that make up the majority of the present-day population. In the 250 years since the first settlers arrived, these islands have been enriched by wanderers from every sea. Merchants have come from India, China, Persia and Burma, and a steady drift of men have retired here, perhaps sharing General Gordon's belief when he visited the Seychelles in 1881, that these islands were the original Garden of Eden.

In the last decade the long isolation of the islands has been broken. Until then only occasional steamships called, either on their way from India to East Africa, or specially to load a cargo of copra. However, in 1972 an international airport was constructed and the Seychelles were now able to offer their beaches and wildlife for the enjoyment of the world's holiday-makers — and with the tourists came independence.

Above Lush vegetation, white sandy beaches and a turquoise sea make Mahé a paradise island.

Zanzibar and Pemba

Zanzibar is one of a pair of equatorial islands off the East African coast, the other being Pemba. Both islands are low-lying and both are humid throughout the year: the onset of the North-East Monsoon in November and the South-West Monsoon in March herald periods of especially heavy rain.

For centuries Zanzibar — with Mombasa on the mainland — was the terminal point of Arab trade with Oman and the Persian Gulf. Sea-going *dhows* arrived with the northeast winds and brought saltfish and carpets. They returned four months later carrying timber and, until the trade was suppressed, slaves. Zanzibar and the adjacent coast were ruled by the Omani Arabs from early in the nineteenth century. They have stamped their influence on its capital, with their distinctive white and

Below The *dhow* wharf at Zanzibar. A ship unloads its cargo.

parapeted houses fronting the harbour and leading to narrow alleys behind. The Arab rulers imported cloves in the early part of the nineteenth century — until then a jealously-guarded monopoly of the East Indies. Though the greater part of the clove crop is grown on Pemba, the storage and marketing is carried out from the town of Zanzibar. The distinctive smell of the spice is as much a part of the town as are its narrow, winding streets and the great, brass-studded doors. Only on the east coast of the islands, where the coral is exposed and the land too poor for plantation, does a small fishing community maintain an independent life-style, based on their graceful, sea-going canoes with double outriggers.

The plantation economy was based on the clove and the coconut. The island peoples were made up of Arab landowners, an immigrant Indian community of bankers and shopkeepers, and a peasant community of the original African stock. As this native community was not large enough to provide all the labour needed for the clove harvest, migrant labour was recruited from the mainland. To them fell also the heavy manual labour of handling the crop from warehouse to ship. It was this despised community of 'mainlanders' who benefitted most from a revolution on the islands in 1964.

Above Graceful outrigger canoes are used for inshore fishing.

Right Loading a tuna fish aboard a bicycle in the town of Zanzibar.

10 MAN AND THE SEA

Fishing

Nearly one-third of the world's population lives on the islands and continents in and around the Indian Ocean. Many of these people do not have enough protein in their diet. Yet despite its size, this great area of water produces only five per cent of the world's fish catch.

Most of the deep water in the Indian Ocean contains few fish. This is because fish and shellfish stay in the shallow water, where they find their food. Tuna fish and whales cross the deep water when they migrate. Big boats come from Japan, France, America and Russia to catch the tuna.

According to the Food and Agriculture Organisation (FAO) of the United Nations, we could catch six times more fish from the Indian Ocean. Many of the nations around the ocean are 'developing nations' and do not have modern boats and equipment. Most of them now claim all the fish inside a line 322 kilometres (200 miles) from the coast. Because some countries have only canoes or small sailing boats, they have asked more 'developed' nations to help them. Countries such as Spain, Russia and Japan may come and catch the fish and take it away. In this case, they would pay a licence fee, or perhaps help the poorer nation to build bigger boats.

The largest fishing nation in this ocean is India, with an annual catch of nearly 250,000 tonnes. Most of this is shrimp, which is exported to America and Europe. Also important for their fish catch are Pakistan, Sri Lanka and South East Africa.

Left Judging by their expressions, these fishermen have caught something rather special.

Above A Japanese fish-freezing vessel moored off Mauritius.

There are very many kinds of fish here, but only some of them are eaten. Some are not good to eat; others live on coral reefs or in mangrove swamps, where they are difficult to catch. The important food fish include tuna, mackerel, and sea bass. In some places the tuna are already being caught faster than they can breed. A hundred years ago, there were many whales in the Indian Ocean. Now they are rare, and whaling boats go to the Antarctic. Even there, the whales are disappearing. This is because men were greedy and caught too many. We must be careful that we do not over-exploit the fish in the Indian Ocean. It is important to plan for the future.

49

Other resources

Around the Indian Ocean are many races and many different climates. There is a great variety of marine life, and many preferences for different foods. We have seen that thousands of tonnes of shrimps and prawns are caught in the Indian Ocean. These are exported at high prices and the money can be used to buy cheaper foods, such as rice.

A few years ago, the FAO carried out a survey to find out how much food could be obtained from the Indian Ocean. They found large quantities of squid (a sort of cuttlefish) and octopus in the warm waters of India, the Persian Gulf, Java and Sri Lanka. Squid and octopus are important foods in many countries, including Spain and Japan.

Another unusual catch is shark, which is eaten in many areas of this ocean. Shark liver contains valuable vitamins, but some fishermen do not understand this, and throw the liver away. Shark fins are dried and sold to Japan and China to make soup.

Not all sea products are eaten. In Sri Lanka, North and West Australia, East Africa and the Persian Gulf, oysters are collected for the mother-of-pearl which lines the inside of their shells. This is used for buttons and decorations. Sometimes a piece of sand or grit becomes lodged inside the oyster, where it becomes covered with hard, white 'nacre'. This is a pearl. If it is a round and perfect shape, it may be very valuable.

The oysters are collected by divers, sometimes wearing just a face mask, sometimes with full diving gear. In Sri Lanka and West Australia, however, the Japanese have helped to set up cultured-pearl stations. Here, oysters are opened wide enough to be 'seeded' with a piece of sand or grit. Often, the oyster will form a pearl around this, called a 'seed pearl'. Although mother-of-pearl buttons have mostly been replaced by plastic, pearl culture is still important.

Another unusual product of the sea is 'bêche-de-mer', or sea cucumber. This is like a sea slug, and is about 10 centimetres long (4 in) and lives on a sandy seabed. In Sri Lanka, men in small boats use face masks to find and gather them. They are dried in the sun and sold as a delicacy, often sliced up and cooked in soup.

Some scientists believe that there are millions of tonnes of small fish in the Indian Ocean, that swim in shoals and are relatively unexploited. It has been suggested that these could be caught in big nets and made into fish meal. This, in turn, could be fed to farm animals. However, such an operation would need big boats, and 'floating factories' to convert the fish into fish meal. So far, no one has risked such a costly experiment.

Right Somalian fishermen inspect their shark catch.

Pollution and desalination

It seems unlikely that the enormous area of the Indian Ocean will become seriously polluted in the near future. Pollution of the sea is caused by industry and by modern farming methods. Neither of these is common in this vast area. Cities pollute the sea with sewage and city waste. Factories empty chemical waste into the sea. Rainwater which drains from big farms may contain insecticides. These are all products of industrial societies, which are rare in the Indian Ocean.

However, more localized pollution from cities and towns may affect shellfish and make them dangerous to eat. Cooking usually makes them safe, but many are placed in special tanks, where they are purified before being sold.

The biggest danger here is probably oil. Much of the world's petroleum comes from Middle East countries in the north-west of the Indian Ocean — Saudi Arabia, Iran and Kuwait. Giant tankers constantly travel from here across the ocean. Some of them carry several hundred thousand tonnes of oil. When one of these is damaged or wrecked, oil drifts to the shore, killing the fish and shellfish on which fishermen depend for their food and their living.

Below The biggest danger of pollution in the Indian Ocean comes from spillages from oil tankers.

Above This complicated system of pipes is a desalination plant.

It is strange that the dry, bare deserts of the Arabian Gulf are surrounded by water. If sea-water could be changed into fresh water and pumped on to the land, deserts could grow food. It is possible to make fresh water from the sea. This is called desalination, and it is done by using heat to turn water into vapour, and then using something cold to turn the vapour back into water. The salt is left behind. In the tropics there is plenty of free heat energy from the sun, but the cost of the desalination machinery is high. This means that the cost of the water would be often too high for the amount of food it could produce.

Many Indian Ocean countries grow fish in freshwater ponds. In far-away Japan, sea fish are grown in netting cages along the shore. This may one day be another way to use the warm waters of the Indian Ocean. Fish would grow quickly here and with plenty of labour available, fish farming could bring prosperity. In the same way, shellfish such as mussels, oysters and scallops could be grown in nets hung from rafts. Japan grows 150,000 tonnes of scallops like this every year. With such a choice of climate, almost anything should be possible in the Indian Ocean.

11 PORTS OF THE INDIAN OCEAN

Colombo

We have seen that many ships from all over the world crisscross the Indian Ocean. They call into ports for loading and unloading cargo, for refuelling and to obtain fresh water, food, and other essential items. Many ports are equipped with deepwater harbours into which very large tankers and ships can safely enter. Nowadays there are many modern facilities for transporting the heavy loads between the docks and the ships, including heavy cranes and other mechanized lifting equipment. You can also see tugs which are used to tow ships, and experienced men called pilots who guide ships safely from the deep sea to the shallow waters of the harbour. Most ports also have dry docks, where repairs can be carried out, and storage areas for cargo.

Colombo is one of the most important ports on the island of Sri Lanka. It is situated on the west coast and if we approached it from the sea from this direction, we would pass palm-fringed beaches and people enjoying the pasttime of fishing. As we approach Colombo itself we would see the black and white lighthouse around which are some dangerous rocks, only a few feet below the sea surface. One such rock is called 'the Drunken Sailor'. On land some of the most impressive buildings are those in 'The Fort' — the site of fortifications originally built by the Portuguese and Dutch. We would also see the dome of the Cathedral.

The harbour was modernized quite recently, and three breakwaters were built to protect it from the rough seas and to provide extra space and berths for ships. Today there are several piers and jetties. At one of these

Left Shipping old and new. An ancient sailing *dhow* and modern cargo ships in Colombo harbour.

Above Modern dock facilities at Colombo.

Right 'Bumboat' salesmen advertise their goods to the passengers of a passing liner.

piers there are pipelines through which large quantities of coconut oil are transported between storage tanks on land and the ships. Other exports include tea, coffee, spices, nuts, and jewellery. Imports include machinery and hardware goods.

Cochin

Another interesting port is Cochin on the west coast of India. Cochin stands on a huge lagoon, fed by water from the Arabian Sea and from rivers flowing into it from the surrounding countryside. During the South-West Monsoon there is heavy rainfall and the rivers carry a considerable amount of water and sediments to the Coast. Cochin's system of inland waterways which runs parallel to the coast is very picturesque. Tourists are able to explore it in river boats. This region has been referred to as 'The Venice of the Arabian Sea'.

Most of the land here is flat and palm-fringed, but densely populated. The fine harbour is able to provide shelter and facilities for a large number of ships and tankers at all times of the year. It is also used by the Indian Navy. Originally the port was developed in the sixteenth century but the harbour was then quite shallow due to constant silting up. In the 1920s channels were dredged and now it is safe for large ships. At Cochin the main imports include mineral oils, chemical fertilizers, copra, and cotton. Exports include iron ore, cashew kernels, tea, rubber, and coconuts.

At the port there are various means of communication with other parts of India, including an airport and railway on Willingdon Island, which forms part of the port. As in other ports throughout the world, ships display flags for signalling which conform to an international code.

Above Weed-covered inland waterways run parallel to the coast around the port of Cochin.

Right Simple ferries carry people to work across one of Cochin's many waterways.

56

12 SHIPS AND SHIPBUILDING
Trade routes across the ocean

Arab dominance in the Indian Ocean was founded on the navigational and meteorological knowledge of their seafarers. This supremacy was to last until the arrival of the Portuguese at the end of the fifteenth century. The skill of the Arab shipbuilders, and the ability of their navigators to use the stars to find their way on long voyages, enabled their merchants to conduct a considerable trade between ports on the northern shores of the Arabian Sea to Zanzibar, Mozambique, Mombasa and other East African ports.

These long ocean voyages were made possible by the North-East and South-West Monsoons which occur without fail every year, and the ocean currents caused by these wind systems. The majority of ships departed from ports along the Gulf of Oman, such as Sohar, Muscat and Qalhat, in the second half of November and early December. They would sail with the winds of the North-East Monsoon to the ports on the coast of East Africa. They would begin their return journey in early April, coasting up to ports in Kenya and aiming to reach the Gulf of Oman before the height of the South-West Monsoon. This monsoon can have very strong winds, and ships tried to avoid being caught at sea when it was at its fiercest.

These early traders also used the monsoons to travel eastwards. Using the north-east winds, they would sail to Malabar, and from there around the southern coast of Sri Lanka to ports in the Malay peninsular. They might then voyage on to the South China Sea in time for the South-West Monsoon, in April or May, to take them to ports in China.

Their return voyage on the North-East Monsoon would begin in about October, and they aimed to arrive in the Malay peninsular by the end of December. In January they would resume their journey to the Gulf ports. During late April or May the first of the South-West Monsoon winds enabled them to sail north-eastwards into the Persian Gulf through the Straits of Hormuz.

Right Running repairs being made on the mast of a *dhow*.

Building a dhow

Above This boatbuilder uses an adze to shape the planks used for the ribs of the boat.

There are a number of different types of Arab sailing craft, all of which are collectively known as *dhows*. Some of these beautiful wooden sailing vessels have features that may well have been adopted from the caravels, with their lateen (triangular) sails, of the early Portuguese explorers.

The hulls of these boats are usually built from a heavy, strong wood called teak, which grows in India and Burma, and from coconut wood from the Maldive and Laccadive Islands. Though modern tools are becoming increasingly common, traditional tools are still in use in many boatyards. These include frame saws, augers for boring holes, and the indispensable adze, a tool used to shape the surface of planks. Originally, a yarn was spun from the bark of the coconut tree and used to sew the planks together. Today iron nails and fastenings have largely taken over from these sewing techniques, but they are still used in smaller craft, such as the outrigger canoes from Sri Lanka and other small fishing vessels.

Dhows' masts are often 20 metres (66 ft) high and have a diameter of one and a half metres. Sails are usually lateen (triangular) in shape, though some lug or rectangular sails are used. Both of these types are 'fore and aft' sails — that is, rigged so that they run down the length of the vessel — like a modern yacht. The sails themselves are very big, with the main sail using about 70 square metres of canvas, and a mizzen (rear) sail about 40 square metres. As a finishing touch, the hulls are treated with a mixture of fish oil and tar or tallow for protection against marine growth. Most ship owners cannot afford to use copper, which is a more efficient method of protection.

Although these unique Arab sailing craft are fast declining in numbers, a considerable number still remain at work along the Indian coast. In 1975 almost a million tonnes of cargo was carried in sailing vessels trading to ports in the Indian sub-continent. In addition to the pure sailing craft the Indian government is today encouraging the building of vessels which are fitted with inboard motors as well as sails. On the Arabian coast many traditional craft have been stripped of sails and fitted with inboard or outboard motors.

It is possible that the shortage of hydro-carbon fuels — coal, petrol and oil — may bring a revival of sailing craft in the Indian Ocean. Many sailors and fishermen still retain the skills to handle such vessels on long coastal, if not ocean, voyages.

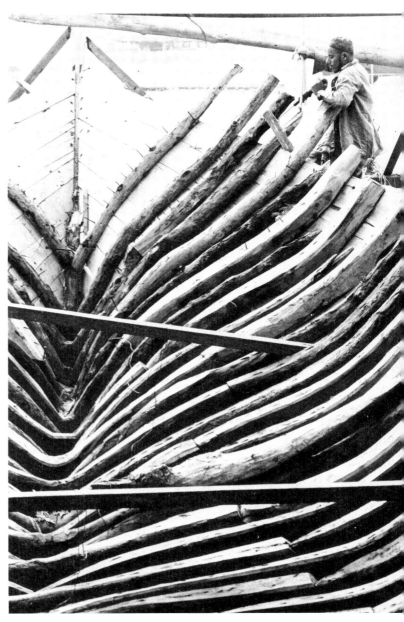

Above The ribs of the *dhow* are fixed in place.

Right The hull of this *dhow* nears completion.

Glossary

Atoll A ring-shaped coral island enclosing a lagoon.

Continental drift The movement of landmasses of the world towards or away from each other.

Continental shelf The part of a continent which lies off-shore and is covered by a shallow layer of of water.

Continental slope The slope joining the end of the continental shelf to the deeper part of the ocean

Coral Stony, skeletal structure formed in masses by simple marine animals (polyps). It is found in various colours and sometimes builds up into coral reefs.

Crustacean Animal usually living in the sea, with a hard shell and many legs. Prawns, crabs and lobsters are all crustaceans.

Current The flow of water in a given direction.

Delta The flat area at the mouth of some rivers, where the mainstream splits up into several tributaries.

Dhows Arab wooden sailing craft, with triangular sails.

Drought A serious lack of rain or water.

Equator An imaginary line making a circle round the earth halfway between the North and South Poles.

Erosion A wearing down or eating away of a substance.

Fossil The remains, impression or trace of an animal or plant found preserved in a rock.

Hurricane A violent tropical wind storm travelling at over 120 km/h.

Icebergs A large mass of ice floating in the colder seas.

Krill Small, shrimp-like animals which form the main food of many whales, seals, penguins and other birds.

Lagoon A shallow, salt-water lake connected to the sea.

Above A row of little boys contemplate the wonders of the Indian Ocean.

Latitude Lines of latitude are imaginary circles around the Earth. They are measured in degrees north and south of the equator.

Mangrove A tree which grows in vast swamps in salty, shallow waters along the tidal marshes. There are several varieties.

Mineral Any substance in the earth or under the sea-bed which can be dug out and used. Coal, iron ore and gold are minerals.

Mollusc A soft animal without a backbone, such as an octopus or a squid. Some (mussels, snails, whelks) have a protective shell.

Monsoon Winds that blow in South Asia,

Salinity Saltiness. The salinity of sea-water varies a little according to the depth of the water and its distance from the Poles.

School A large number of the same kind of fish, swimming about together.

Sediments Clay, sand and silt which collect on the sea floor and may become hard rocks. Remains of dead animals are also incorporated into the sediments.

Tides The rise and fall of the sea which usually occurs twice a day.

Tropics Area on either side of two imaginary circles at equal distances north and south of the equator.

especially in the Indian Ocean, blowing from the south-west in summer (wet), and the north-east in winter (dry).

Nutrients Biochemicals (e.g. nitrate, phosphate) present in sea-water and produced by the decay of dead plants and animals.

Plankton Tiny animals (zooplankton) and plants (phytoplankton) which drift in millions through the seas.

Pollution Contamination of sea-water by dangerous chemicals from industry, oil spillage and sewage, or other rubbish.

Predator A creature that hunts and eats others.

The people who wrote this book

Pat Hargreaves Marine biologist, Institute of Oceanographic Sciences, Surrey.

Dr Robert B. Kidd Marine geologist, Institute of Oceanographic Sciences, Surrey.

Stephen White-Thomson Historian and writer.

Professor G. L. Pickard Professor of Oceanography and Physics, University of British Columbia.

Dr Charles Sheppard Marine biologist, Australian Institute of Marine Science.

Dr Bernard Stonehouse Biologist and specialist in marine birds and animals, Senior Lecturer, University of Bradford.

Dr Brian Rosen Marine biologist, Natural History Musem.

Kenneth Smith C.M.G. H.M. Colonial Service (Rtd.)

H. S. Noel Journalist in fisheries and marine subjects.

Captain N. E. Upham, Ships department, National Maritime Museum.

Books to read

Adam, Robert E., *Oceans of the World* (National Book Co.)

Angel, M. and H., *Ocean Life* (Octopus Books)

Clemons, Elisabeth, *Waves, tides and currents* (A. E. Knopf)

Cochrane, J., *The Amazing World of the Sea* (Angus & Robertson)

Cook, Susannah, *Closer look at Oceans* (F. Watts)

Engel, Leonard, *The Sea* (Time, Life)

Fair, Ruth H., *Shell collectors guide* (C. E. Tuttle)

Gaskell, Thomas F., *The World beneath the Oceans* (Doubleday)

Howard, George, *How we find out about the sea* (Transatlantic)

Keeling, C. H., *Under the Sea* (F. Watts)

Lambert, D., *The Oceans* (Ward Lock)

Merret, N., *The How and Why Wonder Book of the Deep Sea* (Transworld)

Parsons, J., *Oceans* (MacDonald Educationals and Silver Burdett)

Read, Richard, *The living sea* (Penguin)

Ryan, Peter, *The Ocean World* (Penguin)

Saunders, G. D., *Spotters' Guide to Seashells* (Usborne)

Stonehouse, B., *The Living World of the Sea* (Hamlyn)

Index

Picture acknowledgements

Aquila 30, 33 (below); Biofotos 24, 34, 35, 37; Bruce Coleman 26, 31, 41; Colourpix 56-7; James Davis 45, 54, 55 (below); Bill Donohoe 9; Geoslides 7; Ian Griffiths 32, Dr. Wilson/David and Eric Hosking 27; Alan Hutchison *Front cover*, 6, 8 (both), 15, 19 (below), 23, 25, 33 (above), 38, 42, 46, 47 (both), 48, 49, 51, 53 (above), 57 (below), 59, 60, 61, 62-3; Institute of Oceanographic Sciences 14, 22; Anna Jupp 11; Mansell 12, 17, 19 (above); John Mitchell 21, 39; National Institute of Oceanographic Sciences, Goa, India 36; Oxfam 20; Seaphot 28; Seychelles Tourist Information 43; Wayland Picture Library 16, 18, 52; The Weir Group Ltd. 53; Zefa *title page*, 13, 29, 40, 64-5.